# Emil and the Bad Tooth

Read more about Astrid Lindgren and Björn Berg at
rabensjogren.se
astridlindgren.com

Published by Rabén & Sjögren, Stockholm 2016
English translation: Susan Beard 2016
First Edition. Fifth print.
Printed at Livonia Print Ltd, Latvia 2023
ISBN 978-91-29-70091-6

*Rabén & Sjögren is part of*
*Norstedts Förlagsgrupp AB, founded in 1823*

Astrid Lindgren Björn Berg

# EMIL AND THE BAD TOOTH

Translated from Swedish by Susan Beard

rabén&sjögren

On Katthult Farm in Lönneberga, in a place called Småland in Sweden, lived:

*Emil*
a boy who got up to pranks

*Ida*
Emil's sister

*Anton Svensson*
Emil's dad

*Alma Svensson*
Emil's mum

*Lina*
the maid

and *Krösa-Maja*
who sometimes helped at Katthult Farm, but otherwise lived in a little cottage in the woods

*Alfred*
the farmhand

On Katthult Farm there were also:

*cows*

*horses*, one of them was Emil's very own horse called Lukas

*pigs*

*chickens*

*sheep*

and a *cat*

Lina, the girl who was the maid at Katthult Farm, got a toothache one Saturday evening. Wasn't that horrible for her?

Everyone at Katthult Farm was sitting at the kitchen table, having their supper. There was Emil and Emil's dad and Emil's mum and Emil's little sister Ida and Alfred, the farmhand. Oh, and Lina of course, with her toothache!

"Does it hurt very much?" asked little Ida, because she was a kind child.

"Yes, it feels like my head be splittin' open," said Lina.

"I know what you can do," said Alfred, taking his tobacco pouch from his pocket. "Stuff tobacco in your tooth, that'll help!"

So Lina did. But then she shot off to the bin and spat it all out.

“Oh, mercy me!” she cried. “I’d rather have toothache.”

That’s how nasty the tobacco tasted.

“Poor Lina,” said Emil’s mum.

“Yes, poor Lina,” said Emil’s dad.

Emil said nothing because he was thinking about his pranks, the ones he had already got up to, and the ones he hadn’t got up to yet but would as soon as he had the time.

You see, Emil got into mischief every single day.

“I never knowed a child like him,” Lina used to say.

But at this precise moment she wasn’t saying anything. All she could do was groan because her stupid tooth ached and ached.

In the end she picked up a boiling hot potato and popped it into her mouth. That made the tooth hurt ten times worse, just as she knew it would. But she thought it served the tooth right.

“See how that feels,” she said to her tooth. “If you can be nasty, so can I.”

Yes, it was a miserable Saturday evening at Katthult Farm.

And it turned into a miserable night for Lina. She lay on her sofa bed in the kitchen and couldn't sleep because of the terrible pain. And she had to get up at five next morning to milk the Katthult Farm cows. That had to be done on a Sunday just like every other day of the week.

When Lina saw herself in the mirror on the kitchen wall she screamed out loud because, goodness gracious, what a sight she looked! Her right cheek was all swollen, like a big fat bun. Oh, it was just awful! Lina started to cry.

"I look ridiculous," she said to herself.

And it was painful, too.

But off to the field she had to go, because the cows needed milking whether Lina had toothache or not.

She sat there on her milking stool and cried and cried. On this particular Sunday people were coming for coffee at Katthult Farm and Lina loved that kind of thing.

"But I can't let people see me when I'm not the same on both sides," she said, and cried even more.

Just as she was sitting there along came a wasp and stung her on the left cheek, and it swelled up until it was as puffy as the right one.

Now Lina was the same on both sides, but she cried worse than ever. Poor Lina.

When she went back to the farmhouse kitchen and stood in the doorway with her puffed-up cheeks and her eyes all red from crying, everyone jumped in surprise because they had never seen anything so puffy and frightful before.

Emil was having his breakfast. He was just about to drink a mouthful of milk when he noticed Lina over the top of his glass. He burst into giggles and sprayed milk all over his father's best Sunday waistcoat.

"Emil! It's nothing to laugh at," said Emil's mum sternly. She felt sorry for Lina. And probably Emil did too. But he laughed at all sorts of things, that boy, even when he shouldn't.

"Poor Lina," said Emil's mum. "You look such a sight you can't possibly show yourself to anyone. Emil, you'll have to run over to Krösa-Maja and ask her to come and help serve the coffee and cakes."

Emil's mum and dad were about to leave for church. They went every Sunday. Alfred hitched the horse to the wagon and away they went, while Emil ran off obediently to Krösa-Maja's cottage.

When he got home again Lina was sitting on the kitchen steps. She was still crying because her tooth wouldn't stop aching. Alfred and little Ida stood there and didn't know what to do with her.

"Looks like you'll be going to Per the Blacksmith after all," said Alfred.

It was Per the Blacksmith who pulled out bad teeth with his long, horrible pliars.

"How much do he charge for pulling out a tooth?" asked Lina.

"One krona an hour," said Alfred.

But then Emil said:

"I dare say I can get that tooth out cheaper and quicker. I know a way."

He had it all planned.

"I only need two things: Lukas and some strong thread. I'll wind the thread round your tooth, Lina, and tie the other end to my belt. Then I'll gallop off on Lukas and *plop*, out flies your tooth.

“I’ll give you *plop*,” said Lina. “There’ll be no galloping around with me, thank you very much!”

But her tooth went on hurting, and finally she said with a sigh:

“Oh, all right, let’s give it a try.”

So Emil led Lukas to the kitchen steps and when they had sorted out the business with the thread, up he jumped onto his horse. Behind them stood poor Lina, firmly attached to the thread. No wonder she was scared!

“Now all we’re waiting for is the *plop*,” said Alfred.

Emil set off at a gallop.

"Ooh, not long now," said little Ida.

But there was no *plop*, because someone else started galloping, and that someone was Lina. She was so afraid of a *plop* that she ran as fast as Lukas. Emil shouted at her to stop, but Lina ran and ran, and of course the thread was so loose there simply couldn't be a *plop*.

This isn't working, thought Emil. But that tooth is coming out, and I'm the one to do it. So he sped towards a fence, and with a leap Lukas flew over. Lina followed, scared out of her wits, and guess what? She flew over as well. A *plop* wasn't something she wanted to hear.

But afterwards she was ashamed for spoiling everything, because she still had her tooth and it was hurting worse than ever.

"I'll have to think of a different way," said Emil.

"Yes. One that don't go so fast," said Lina. "Why yank the tooth out with a *plop*? Can't you sort of slide it out?"

Then Emil came up with a bright idea. He made Lina sit on the ground under the old pear tree and he tied her tightly to it with some rope.

"Try running away now," he said. He picked up the end of the thread, which was dangling from Lina's mouth, and took it to the grinding wheel, the one his dad used to sharpen axes for chopping wood and scythes for cutting hay. The grinding wheel was turned by a handle, and it was to that very handle that Emil tied the thread. Yes, he really did, because he planned to wind out Lina's tooth.

"It won't be one of those quick *plops*, more a kind of *drrr*. Slowly, like you wanted," he said.

Little Ida shuddered. She was so glad she didn't have a tooth that had to be wound out with a *drrr*.

Emil started to turn the handle. The thread got tighter and tighter, and the tighter it got, the more terrified Lina became. She was as scared of a *drrr* as she was of a *plop*.

"But she can't run away, luckily," thought Emil.

"Soon it will go *drrr*," said Little Ida.

But then Lina screamed:

"Stop! I don't want to!"

And quick as a flash she pulled a small pair of scissors out of her apron pocket, and cut off the thread.

Afterwards she was ashamed again, and sad too, because she really *did* want to get rid of the tooth. But Emil said:

"Keep your rotten old tooth! I've done what I can."

Then Lina cried and said if only Emil would have one more go, she wouldn't try anything stupid again.

And because he was so kind, Emil agreed to have another go. Alfred and Ida thought that was a good idea too.

"I still think a quick way is best," said Emil. "But it has to be one you can't spoil, even if you *do* get scared."

And very soon Emil had worked out a plan.

"We climb up to the roof of the barn and then you jump down onto the haystack underneath. Half way down the tooth will fly out — *plop*."

"Only you, Emil, could come up with something so diabolically awful," said Lina.

But because her tooth was aching very, very badly she finally followed Emil up onto the roof of the barn, where he hammered a large nail into the corner of the roof and tied the thread to it.

"Go on, jump," he said.

Alfred and Little Ida stood on the ground, waiting for Lina to come sailing down from above. But Ida covered her eyes with her hands because she didn't dare to watch.

And, as a matter of fact, Lina didn't dare to jump.

"Ooh, I can't," she wailed. "I don't dare, and that's the truth."

"I'll lend you a hand, then," said Emil, kind boy that he was.

He jabbed Lina in the back and with a cry she leapt from the roof.

But the only *plop* to be heard was the nail coming out. Not the tooth. Lina still had that, as she sat in the haystack where she had landed. And now she was in a rage with Emil.

"Pranks you can do, no trouble. But pull out teeth? Huh, you're no good at that."

It was a good job Lina was angry because it made her march straight to Per the Blacksmith who pulled out her tooth with his enormous, horrible pliars. *Plop*, it went. Lina took the tooth and threw it onto Per the Blacksmith's rubbish heap, and then she went home to Katthult Farm, happy and satisfied, and with no toothache.

Perhaps Emil couldn't pull out teeth, but he could invent interesting games. And now he was pretending to be little Ida's doctor, seeing as he couldn't be a dentist any longer.

Little Ida had to lie in her bed while Emil looked in her mouth and listened to her breathing, just like the doctor did.

“What kind of disease have I got?” asked Little Ida.

“You’ve got typhis,” said Emil. “That’s a terrible disease.”

It was Krösa-Maja who had told him how awful typhus could be, and how you could catch it from other people. And when you got the disease your face turned all blue, so Krösa-Maja said. That’s why Emil took some of his mother’s writing ink and painted Ida with it. Naturally he wanted her to have exactly the right colour.

“Now I’ll show you what typhis is, Ida,” he said. “But squeeze your eyes shut so you don’t get ink in them.”

Just at that moment Krösa-Maja arrived to help with the coffee party, and she was absolutely horrified when she saw Ida looking so dreadful and so blue.

“What in all the world!” shrieked Krösa-Maja.

“It’s typhis,” said Emil, with a grin.

That very minute Emil’s mum and dad came back from church, and all their guests as well, with the vicar leading the way.

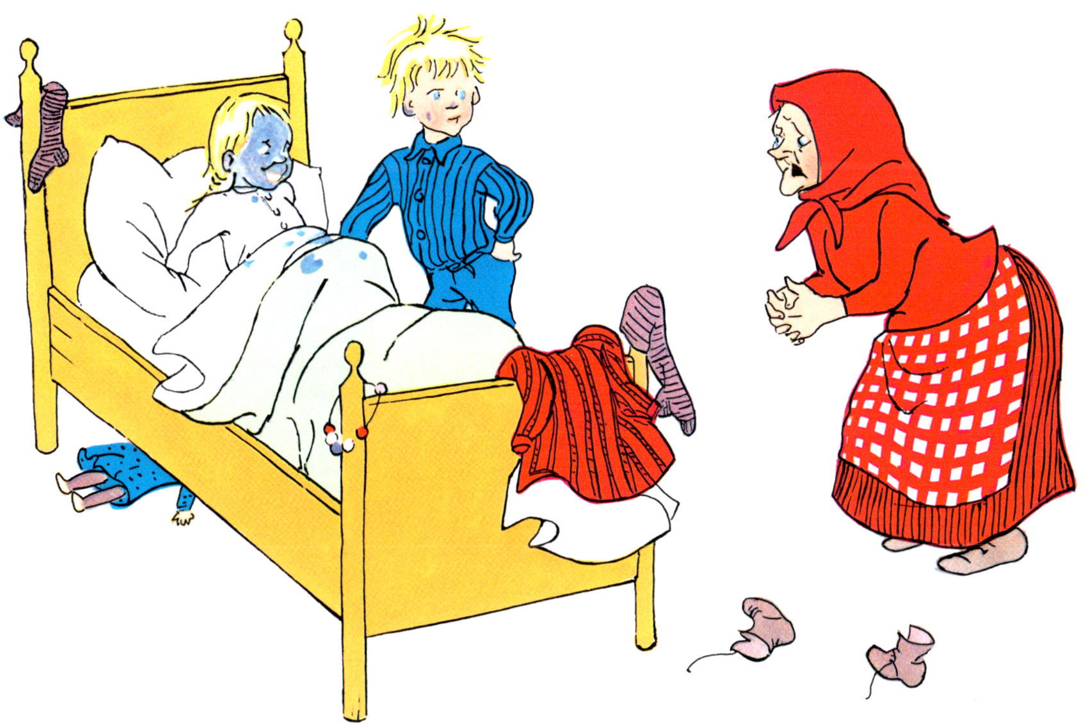

Krösa-Maja stood on the front steps, shouting at the top of her voice:

"Be off with you! Be off with you! We've typhis at the farm!"

But Emil's mum said:

"What are you on about? Who's got typhus?"

Then little Ida poked her head out from behind Krösa-Maja.

"Me," she said, and she burst out laughing.

Then everyone began to laugh. Everyone except Emil's dad. He bawled:

"Where's Emil?"

Because he realised, of course, that this was one of Emil's pranks.

But Emil had hidden himself in the log box and didn't want to talk to his dad right at that moment.